Careers in Construction

Architect

Cathleen Small

Cavendish
Square
New York

Published in 2016 by Cavendish Square Publishing, LLC
243 5th Avenue, Suite 136, New York, NY 10016

Website: cavendishsq.com

This publication represents the opinions and views of the author based on his or her personal experience, knowledge, and research. The information in this book serves as a general guide only. The author and publisher have used their best efforts in preparing this book and disclaim liability rising directly or indirectly from the use and application of this book.

CPSIA Compliance Information: Batch #CW16CSQ

All websites were available and accurate when this book was sent to press.

Library of Congress Cataloging-in-Publication Data

Small, Cathleen, author.
Architect / Cathleen Small.
pages cm. — (Careers in construction)
Includes bibliographical references and index.
ISBN 978-1-5026-0974-8 (hardcover) ISBN 978-1-5026-0975-5 (ebook)
1. Architectural practice. 2. Architecture. I. Title.

NA1995.S63 2016
720—dc23

2015027605

Editorial Director: David McNamara
Editors: Andrew Coddington and Kelly Spence
Copy Editor: Rebecca Rohan
Art Director: Jeffrey Talbot
Designer: Alan Sliwinski
Senior Production Manager: Jennifer Ryder-Talbot
Production Editor: Renni Johnson
Photo Research: J8 Media

Printed in the United States of America

Table of Contents

The Sky Garden, with its large windows and stunning views, is London's highest public garden.

Introduction

Nearly as long as humans have lived on the Earth, the field of construction has existed. Obviously, it wasn't always formally defined, but even back in the earliest days of mankind, cave dwellers sought shelter that would meet their specific needs for safety, warmth, and proximity to food and water. Later, as humans began to use tools, housing became more than just searching for the appropriate cave. Structures arose from the materials available—clay, mud, straw, and even ice. These structures may have been primitive by our current standards, but the fact remains that they were constructed by people and with a purpose.

In the twenty-first century, construction is often thought of as a **blue-collar** field. We think of men and women in hard hats working at construction sites, pounding in nails, fitting pipes, wiring buildings for electricity, and tasks of that nature. And indeed, many jobs in the construction field are blue-collar in nature. However, there is a **white-collar** side to construction, too—there are men and women working primarily in offices behind the scenes. There are businesspeople and accountants and salespeople and assistants ... and then there are the architects.

How could we forget about the architects? Other people come and go throughout a project's life cycle, but the architects work from the very beginning stages of the project and see it through to the end. A building or structure starts with an architect and ends with an architect, even though it is touched by many others along the way.

Every job in the field of construction is important; without one piece, the entire puzzle is incomplete. But without the architect, there is truly no project, for the architect is the person who conceives of and develops the idea—often with input from the client, but sometimes just in his or her own mind. The architect is the person who combines the science of structure and form with the **aesthetics** of art and nature to create a structure that both serves a purpose and pleases the eye.

But architects are more than faceless people at the head of a project, scribbling designs on sketchpads and creating mockups of buildings, bridges, and landscapes with an ease that makes it seem almost like magic. Rather, architects are often the face of a project, meeting with clients and overseeing all aspects. Their job may start in an office, but it takes them to client meetings, to construction sites, and anywhere else the project demands.

An architect's duties are numerous and sometimes tedious, but the rewards are great. This is a field for people who have a passion for design and creativity, as well as a logical mind that can meld the artistic side of design with the methodical side of form. Architects are historians who draw on the designs of the past for inspiration and for solid architectural practices, but they are also forward-thinking pioneers who constantly find new, sometimes better or more striking, ways to create.

Architecture is a field for those who have vision and want to see that vision come to life. And it's a field for people who aren't afraid to work hard and to learn from those who've come before them when they're finding their own niche.

The Neoclassical United States Capitol building is one of the country's most recognizable structures.

CHAPTER 1

Architecture: From Its Beginnings to the Modern Era

Although it may not have been officially called *architecture*, there has never been a time in human history when architecture wasn't a job. Shelter has always been a basic human need, and even the earliest cave dwellers carefully chose their shelter based on its functionality, location, and suitability for their needs.

However, the ancient Egyptians may have been the first civilization to actually use the principles of architecture as we now know it—craftsmen carefully used architectural principles to design the tombs and burial chambers that we recognize as the pyramids. However, before we talk more about the history of architecture, let's establish exactly what architecture is.

What Is Architecture?

Most simply put, architecture is art and science combined to carefully design and construct buildings or other physical structures. Young children first explore the principles of architecture when they use blocks to build towers. Even very young children quickly learn that putting a large block on top of a stack of small blocks will generally result in a tower collapse! Later, many children continue to explore the world of architecture with toys such as Legos, which allow them to create more architecturally complex buildings. With basic blocks, children must rely mostly on size and structure to create a tower, but with Legos they add an ability to connect pieces into the mix. What seems like a simple childhood toy set is actually a primitive form of architectural tools.

In the adult professional world, architecture naturally gets far more complex. Architects consider function, technology, environment, and aesthetics, among other factors, when they design and plan a structure. Further complicating the task of an architect is that these factors are often intertwined. For example, architects have to consider the many possible building materials they want to use in the context of environment and aesthetics. Bricks may be a lovely idea for the exterior of a building and may be aesthetically pleasing, but if the structure will be in an earthquake-prone environment, bricks are *not* a good choice. Architects undertake specialized and rigorous study to learn how to take all of these factors into consideration and create a functional, stable, and attractive structure.

The History of Architecture

Just as written books and stories evolved from verbal storytelling traditions, architecture has evolved from what is known as **vernacular architecture**. In vernacular architecture, builders create structures based on local traditions and needs and using local materials. Although vernacular architecture still exists in the twenty-first century, it's often thought of with respect to primitive shelters or housing among **indigenous** peoples. The term vernacular architecture is thought to have been coined in the early 1800s, but the concept has been around for much longer. In the days before people hired professional architects to design homes and buildings, people used their local environment and landscape considerations to inform how they would build their homes. The Inuit, for example, built igloos for temporary shelter from snow. Ice and snow were readily available, and by using the ice to construct a dome-shaped shelter, the Inuit could create an environment in which to survive harsh winter conditions.

The Inuit also built turf huts, which were more permanent dwellings that used local stones and turf to create a livable shelter. Some Native American tribes built their homes into cliffs using readily available stones and adobe mortar, as well as large crossbeams. Their location in the sides of cliffs acted as a means of protection from potential invasions from neighboring tribes. The architecture of these dwellings was remarkable—in the southwestern United States, cliff dwellings built in the twelfth century are still intact.

The Pueblo tribe lived in cliff dwellings at Mesa Verde from 600 to 1300 CE. Their dwellings still stand today.

Beyond vernacular architecture, ancient civilizations began to develop architecture with a close eye on art. Many examples of ancient architecture, such as those found in Egypt, **Mesopotamia**, Asia, and the Middle East, were developed for religious purposes. As such, aesthetics were key. The buildings needed to inspire the public but also pay **homage** to the gods. Further, some of these structures, such as the Egyptian pyramids, the Parthenon in Greece, and the Gothic cathedrals of Europe, were designed to showcase art.

Egyptian Architecture

Ancient Egypt is famed for the pyramids, which were built as burial tombs but which also showcased early Egyptian art and stories in murals, paintings, and **hieroglyphics**. The oldest pyramids were built thousands of years ago and are considered architectural marvels partly because their simple design of posts, **lintels**, and stone has stood the test of time.

Sumerian Architecture

Around the same time period, the Sumerians in Mesopotamia and Persia were designing similar pyramid structures called **ziggurats**. However, instead of being used as tombs, ziggurats were designed to bring people closer to the gods.

Asian Architecture

Early Asian architecture was also influenced by religion. Asia is a vast region that encompasses peoples from a number of different religions, including Buddhism, Hinduism, and Sikhism, and the early architecture of Asia showcases that diversity. For example, followers of **pantheistic** religions, who believe that everything, including nature, combines to form an all-encompassing god, designed buildings that enhanced the nature around them.

Celtic Architecture

Although much of European architecture dates to later, there are examples of early Stone Age architecture in northern Europe, such as Stonehenge in England. Stonehenge and similar structures are known as **megaliths** and were built from large stones. They are thought to have had a religious significance, although some also appear to have a connection to the field of astronomy.

Minoan Architecture

Similarly, ancient Greek and Minoan architecture also dates back to the period before the birth of Christ on the Christian calendar. Minoan architecture was found on the island of Crete, but unfortunately, much of it was destroyed by earthquakes thousands of years ago.

Greek Architecture

Ancient Greek architecture also dates to before the birth of Christ but later than Minoan architecture, and more of it still stands. Inspired by the Egyptians, the Greeks created stone structures from limestone and marble, among other elements, and they used posts and lintels for architectural support. They also employed the use of columns for structural support, and many existing ancient Greek structures showcase those columns.

Like their predecessors, the Greeks created religious structures, but they also built municipal buildings, stadiums, and theaters. An ancient Greek structure that still stands today is the Parthenon (a former religious temple), part of the Acropolis (an ancient **citadel**).

Roman Architecture

Ancient Roman architecture is also well known and in fact borrowed heavily from Greek architecture. Several examples of ancient Roman architecture still stand today, including the Colosseum (a concrete and stone amphitheater completed in the year 80 CE) and the Roman aqueducts. The aqueducts are a significant symbol of early Roman architecture because they were technologically groundbreaking. Inadequate drainage was a problem in the urban Roman areas, and the architects' solution

The Pont du Gard in the Languedoc-Roussillon region of France is a magnificent example of the Roman aqueduct system.

was to design elaborate drainage systems and aqueducts. The Romans also built aqueduct bridges, such as the three-tiered Pont du Gard, which was built in the first century CE and is still standing in France; and municipal facilities, including amphitheaters and public baths.

Ancient Roman architecture was grand and imposing, but it was also innovative in terms of functionality. The aqueduct system solved the water needs for urban areas, but it wasn't the only groundbreaking feature the Romans contributed to the field of architecture. The Romans also used arches and roof domes as a means of support for their buildings. Arches meant that structures such as bridges required fewer support columns than used in the designs of their predecessors, the Greeks, and domed roofs allowed the Romans to build larger covered areas than before.

The Romans also gave us concrete, which is a mixture of mortar, sand, water, and stones. Previously, architecture had relied heavily on marble and other stone, but the invention of concrete gave the Romans more options for strong, durable building materials. Concrete also gave the Romans more flexibility in their designs, which led to a new aesthetic in architecture.

Byzantine Architecture

The Romans' architectural innovations led to **Byzantine** architecture, starting around 330 CE. Byzantine architecture was based in what is now Istanbul, in Turkey. At that time, it was the capital of the Roman Empire, and thus many Byzantine architects were Italians who had relocated from their home country.

Byzantine era architecture used **pendentives**, which were concave triangular sections that enabled architects to put a circular dome on top of a square room. Byzantine architects also used art and elaborate glass mosaics to decorate their structures.

Although Byzantine architecture was initially inspired by Roman architecture, it went through several periods and eventually became more influenced by eastern traditions. This meant that later Byzantine buildings were more geometrically complex and used brick and plaster for decorative purposes. Later Byzantine architecture eventually influenced the designs in early Islamic architecture, as well as the architecture in Orthodox eastern European countries.

Romanesque Architecture

After the collapse of Rome, western Europe also saw the emergence of the Romanesque style of architecture. In France, Germany, Italy, and Spain, Romanesque architecture appeared around the eleventh century CE. Romanesque architecture is characterized by buildings that are massive in scale—a response to Europe's newfound political and economic stability.

Romanesque architecture was heavily influenced by Christianity, and many new Romanesque churches and cathedrals were built, including the famous Leaning Tower of Pisa, which was a bell tower for the Cathedral of Pisa.

While the Greeks were known for their aesthetic sensibility in architecture and the Romans were known for their innovative engineering, the Romanesque architects were known for neither. Many Roman building techniques were lost, and the Romanesque architects went back to relatively primitive design features, such as thick walls, narrow windows (which resulted in dim interiors), simple design lines, and roof-supporting vaults and buttresses.

This Romanesque tower, with its narrow windows, leans over Pisa, Italy.

Gothic Architecture

Romanesque architecture was followed by Gothic architecture in the mid-twelfth century. Like Romanesque architects, Gothic architects used vaults and **flying buttresses** for roof support. However, they also used thinner walls and huge stained-glass windows, which made their buildings brighter than the buildings of the Romanesque era. Moreover, they were known for using pointed arches in their designs, which are thought to have been inspired by early Islamic architecture.

Gothic architecture is often seen in cathedrals. It was not a religious architectural movement per se, but Gothic architects did introduce ideas about how this new style of architecture could enhance religious devotion, and much of the money used to build these new cathedrals came from **monastic** orders and local bishops.

The pointed arches used in Gothic architecture allowed architects to build ceilings at a much steeper angle than before, which created a feeling of buildings that soared toward the heavens.

Perhaps the best-known example of Gothic architecture is Notre Dame Cathedral in Paris, which was completed in 1345. Other well-known examples of Gothic architecture include the Cologne Cathedral in Germany (which

Notre Dame Cathedral in Paris is an awe-inspiring example of Gothic architecture, with its magnificent flying buttresses which are visible from the River Seine.

took more than six hundred years to complete!) and Westminster Abbey in London.

Renaissance Architecture

Around 1400, the Renaissance came to Europe, and it affected the field of architecture by resurrecting architectural styles from ancient Rome. The dome of the Florence Cathedral is thought to be the first example of Renaissance architecture.

However, Renaissance architecture wasn't solely based on ancient Roman architecture. It borrowed from ancient Greek, Byzantine, and Gothic architecture as well. Renaissance buildings often had complex domes and towers, but aesthetically architects added a new dimension to their designs by using mosaics, stained glass, and **fresco** murals. Michelangelo Buonarroti, famed painter of the ceiling of the Sistine Chapel and sculptor of the statue of David, was considered a leading Renaissance architect.

Baroque Architecture

Renaissance architecture was followed by Baroque in the mid-1500s, which arose out of religious reform and turmoil occurring across Europe. As Protestantism threatened to spread across Europe, the Roman Catholic Church launched a movement to attract people away from Protestantism and back to Catholicism. Part of this movement was a renewed emphasis on the arts, which inspired the Baroque era's more dramatic, complex, grand architectural features.

Baroque architecture is elaborate and heavily ornamented with features of light, color, and texture. Baroque churches featured showy facades and domes, and

This Renaissance cathedral's dome dominates the skyline in Florence, Italy.

ceilings covered in frescos. Baroque architects wanted to dazzle people with the splendor of their buildings. One interesting artistic feature of Baroque design is the use of **trompe l'oeil** art, which used visual illusion to create 3-D effects.

Perhaps the best-known example of Baroque architecture is Saint Peter's Square in Rome, which was designed around the Renaissance-built St. Peter's Basilica. The square is grand in scale, and the colonnades that ring the square are designed to look as though visitors are being drawn into the Basilica by the embracing arms of the church.

Neoclassical Architecture

Baroque architecture demonstrated excess, but at the same time, the early beginnings of Neoclassical architecture answered that excess with a simpler style. St. Paul's Cathedral in London, designed by famed architect Christopher Wren, is a well-known example of Neoclassical architecture. The cathedral is a working church that receives countless visitors a day to see its famous dome, but it is particularly well known as being the church where England's Prince Charles and Lady Diana Spencer wed in 1981.

Neoclassical architecture was simpler than Baroque in style, but it also featured a return to the principles of early Greek and Roman architecture. Neoclassical buildings were huge in size and featured columns or pillars supporting Renaissance-style domes. However, this era also introduced the architectural innovations of layered **cupolas** and inner cores, which allowed Neoclassical architects to build bigger, grander structures.

Neoclassical architecture began in Paris, and one well-known example from this time period is Paris's Arc de Triomphe, designed by Jean Chalgrin in 1806. However, Neoclassical architecture quickly spread beyond Paris to Sweden, Germany, Russia, and the United States.

Jean Chalgrin designed Paris's Neoclassical Arc de Triomphe which is located on the Champs-Élysées.

In the United States, the US Capitol building is probably the best-known representation of Neoclassical architecture. It was begun in 1793 but not completed until the mid-1800s. Its design was inspired by the Pantheon in Rome and parts of the Louvre Museum in Paris, and it was heavily influenced by President Thomas Jefferson, who was a fan of the Neoclassical style.

Nineteenth- and Twentieth-Century Architecture

The nineteenth century was a time of architectural revival in the United States and in Europe. Architectural styles from this century included Greek Revival, Gothic Revival, Neo-Romanesque Revival, and Beaux-Arts architecture, which revived and combined the Renaissance and Baroque styles. Late in the century, Art Nouveau architecture appeared and brought elements of nature into architecture, such as in Paris's Metro stations, which featured elaborate designs that appeared to resemble bean shoots and seedpods.

In the mid-1800s, two significant events occurred in American architectural history: Frank Lloyd Wright was born, and the skyscraper was designed. Frank Lloyd Wright is probably the best-known American architect. He was born in 1867, and by the early 1900s he was establishing himself as a powerful name in the field. Wright redesigned how Americans thought of architectural space and introduced the open-plan layout, which is incredibly common even now, nearly a century later. He also used natural materials in his building. Wright designed the Guggenheim Museum in New York in the late 1950s, but he may be even better known for Fallingwater, a Pennsylvania home that Wright designed over a waterfall for his clients. What's extraordinary about Fallingwater's design is that it appears to stretch out over the waterfall with no apparent support in places. Obviously, it *is* supported, but that's the beauty and

The Frank Lloyd Wright–designed Fallingwater house appears to float above a natural waterfall.

I. M. Pei: International Style
(April 26, 1917–)

I. M. Pei is a Chinese-born American architect who may be best known as the designer of the controversial glass pyramid outside the Louvre Museum in Paris. He was born in Guangzhou, China, and moved to the United States at the age of eighteen to attend the University of Pennsylvania, Philadelphia. He later transferred to the Massachusetts Institute of Technology to study in their architectural engineering program. He graduated in 1939. However, he could not return to China because World War II was going on at that time. Instead, he worked on architectural contracts in Boston, New York City, and Los Angeles with a unit of the National Defense Research Committee. After the war ended, he became an assistant professor in the Graduate School of Design at Harvard and taught until 1948, when he became director of the architectural division of Webb & Knapp in New York City. Working with developer William Zeckendorf, Pei created the Mile High Center in Denver in 1955; the Hyde Park Redevelopment in Chicago in 1959; and the Place Ville-Marie in Montreal in 1965.

In 1955, a year after becoming a United States citizen, Pei formed the architectural firm of I. M. Pei & Associates. Under the firm's name, Pei designed such famous buildings as the Luce Memorial Chapel in Taiwan; the Mesa Laboratory of the National Center for Atmospheric Research in Boulder, Colorado;

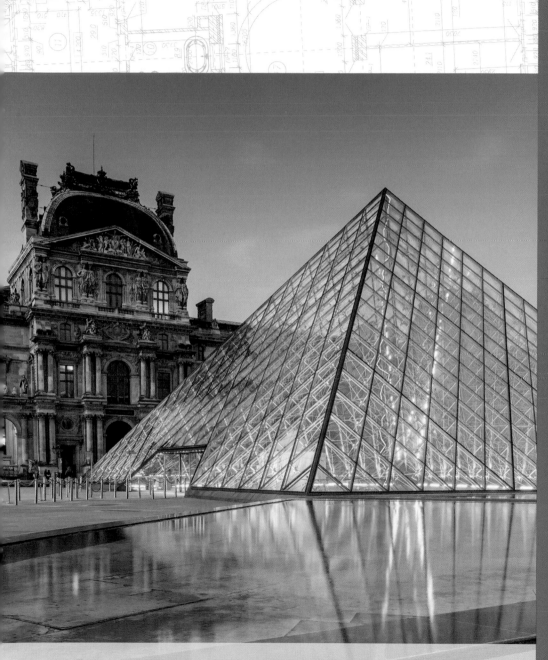

The pyramid outside the Louvre Museum in Paris is a jewel in I. M. Pei's architectural design crown.

I. M. Pei: International Style
(April 26, 1917–)

and the Everson Museum of Art in Syracuse, New York. Pei also designed the pentagonal control tower seen in many US airports. In 1960, Pei was also chosen to design a new terminal at the busy John F. Kennedy International Airport in New York City, and in 1964 Jackie Kennedy chose Pei to design the John F. Kennedy Memorial Library at Harvard University.

One of Pei's finest designs is thought to be the East Building at the National Gallery of Art in Washington, DC, built in 1978. It's a triangular composition, which is a form Pei returned to in the 1980s, when he designed the glass pyramid for the courtyard of the Louvre—a design that ended up being rather controversial and mocked by many architectural critics who found it not fitting for the style of the museum and referred to it, among other things, as an "annex to Disneyland."

From the 1970s to the turn of the millennium, Pei continued to design notable structures, including the New York City Convention Center, Dallas Symphony Hall, the Gateway office complex in Singapore, the John Hancock Tower in Boston, the Indiana University Museum, the west wing of the Boston Museum of Fine Arts, the Nestle Corporation Headquarters, the El Paso Tower, the Beijing Fragrant Hill Hotel, and the Miho Museum in Japan.

Despite his advanced age and the fact that he officially retired from his firm in 1990, Pei has continued to design buildings in the 2000s. He designed 2008's Suzhou Museum in China and the offshore Museum of Islamic Art in Qatar.

Pei's work is known as an extension of the International Style, with its rectangular forms and irregular silhouettes. He skillfully arranges groups of geometric shapes and uses richly contrasting materials, spaces, and surfaces. Pei has received numerous awards for his work, including the Pritzker Architecture Prize in 1983, the Presidential Medal of Freedom a decade later, a lifetime achievement award from the Cooper-Hewitt Museum another decade later, and the Royal Gold Medal from the Royal Institute of British Architects in 2010, at the tender age of ninety-three. He is also an officer of the Legion of Honor, a premier order of the French republic that was originally established by Napoleon Bonaparte.

innovation of Wright's design—the home appears to float in the air over the waterfall.

Despite the overlapping time period, Wright was not heavily involved in the design of skyscrapers. That distinction goes to William Le Baron Jenney, an architect and engineer who founded the Chicago School of Architecture. Skyscraper architecture began in the mid-1800s, and skyscrapers now dominate the skyline of most major cities in the United States. Chicago was not the only city developing skyscrapers, though; New York City was also experiencing rapid growth in the number of skyscrapers during this period, with buildings such as the Empire State Building, the Chrysler Building, and Rockefeller Center being constructed. The Empire State Building, the Chrysler Building, and the entrance to Rockefeller Center are all part of the Art Deco movement of the 1920s and 1930s, which emphasized building with highly decorative elements as well as elements from ancient art.

The twentieth century is also known for Revivalist architecture, which basically describes a period when architects drew inspiration from past architectural movements, such as Romanesque, Gothic, and Beaux-Arts. Well-known Revivalist buildings constructed in the twentieth century include the Pennsylvania Railway

Station (commonly referred to simply as Penn Station) in New York City; the Lincoln Memorial in Washington, DC; Hearst Castle in California; and the Louvre's glass pyramid in Paris, constructed by I. M. Pei.

Those architects who were not Revivalists in the early twentieth century were often Modernists. They used the most current building materials and techniques, and their work tended to include a lot of iron, steel, concrete, and glass. Functionality was the end goal in these Modernist structures.

Over in Europe, though, some architects didn't care for the Modernist style and instead practiced Expressionist architecture, which included lots of asymmetrical elements, curves, and spirals. One famous example is the Sydney Opera House in Australia, whose roof was reportedly designed to look like the sails of a ship coming into the harbor.

World War II also influenced architecture, particularly in Europe. "Social housing" began to spring up in the form of apartment blocks of low-cost housing. These apartments were functional but not particularly aesthetically pleasing; they were simple and served a purpose.

As the world emerged from the grips of World War II, the International Style of modern architecture became popular, with its sleek designs of steel and glass. It was often used in skyscrapers but also for corporate office blocks. This style remained prevalent until around 1970, when High-Tech architecture became popular. The glass and steel of Modernist architecture were still used in High-Tech architecture, along with other light metals and plastic derivatives. High-Tech architecture was focused on using cutting-edge technology to design buildings and other structures.

Architecture Now

While styles change with the times, one thing has not changed since the beginnings of architecture: it has always been influenced by external factors, such as art, religion, politics, and environment. The prevalent style of art at any given time in history can be seen reflected in that period's architecture, and for many years the dominant religious traditions of the time could also be seen. Politics has long played a role in architecture, too, with regions wanting to demonstrate their political structure and power through the buildings erected. Nowadays, in the early twenty-first century, environment plays a big role in an architect's craft. We are heavily focused on renewable resources and ways that we can borrow from the environment without destroying it. For example, wood has long been used as a building material, but as we're seeing the depletion of our forests, architects are implementing other building strategies that decrease our dependence on wood as a building material. Bamboo, for example, is being touted as a good flooring substitute for wood because bamboo grows quickly and is readily available.

Always, architects are ever mindful of Mother Nature. California, for example, regularly experiences drought conditions and earthquakes, so architects are implementing features in their buildings, such as low-flush toilets, gray-water recycling systems, and flexible building materials, to combat these problems and help minimize devastation. Homes in tornado-prone areas of the Midwest, on the other hand, are built with strong basements in which families can seek shelter if a tornado hits. In hurricane-prone areas, architects work within strict building codes designed to ensure the maximum possible safety in hurricane-force winds.

Being an architect is not as simple as designing with a mind to form and function. Instead, the master architect must consider aesthetics, environment, materials, function, innovation, and classic design to inform his or her creation of a new structure. It's an ever-changing field that challenges and inspires those who choose to pursue it.

The Dubai skyline with its modern skyscrapers glitters along the edge of the Persian Gulf.

CHAPTER 2

Starting a Career in Architecture

Up until the late 1800s, anyone with a talent in architecture could begin a career in the field simply by working as an apprentice or by independently reading about and studying the craft. There were no established guidelines or standards. However, in the mid-1800s, a number of prominent architects in the United States formed the American Institute of Architects (AIA). The AIA wasn't a licensing agency; rather, it established standards and professionalism in the field. The AIA supported such early architectural schools as MIT, Cornell, University of Illinois, and Columbia University. In supporting these schools, the AIA was able to ensure that architects coming from these programs were well trained in the standards of the craft.

General Interests

It's not unusual to assume that to be an architect, you have to be good at drawing. However, that assumption is false. Sure, being talented at drawing is helpful, but it's not required. When an architect creates a drawing, it's not meant to necessarily be beautiful—it's meant to communicate design. In reality, even a rough sketch can

Being good at drawing helps in a career in architecture—but surprisingly, it's not absolutely necessary.

communicate design. Rather, it's more important to have design sense in terms of structure and form. Influential twentieth-century architect Lou Kahn once said, "An artist can make a cart with square wheels, but an architect can't." There's a lot of truth in that statement: architects must understand form and function to create, and they must communicate that in their drawings … but those drawings need not be works of art.

The ability to design is what's most important in architecture. If you were the kid who would spend hours building elaborate skyscrapers and bridges out of your Legos, architecture might be for you. If you were the kid who stared at buildings under construction and wondered what those big girders were used for, architecture might be for you. If you designed elaborate dioramas for your elementary-school book reports, architecture might be for you.

If you think you might be interested in becoming an architect, there are areas of study you can pursue. While in high school, you can take classes in English, history, humanities, math, and physics to help prepare you for a career in architecture. You may also want to take art classes, such as drawing, painting, sculpting, or photography, to prepare you for later studies and an eventual career in architecture. Computer classes will also

CHRISTOPHER WREN: CATHEDRAL ARCHITECT (OCTOBER 20, 1632–FEBRUARY 25, 1723)

Sir Christopher Wren, who was knighted in 1673, was an astronomer and mathematician, as well as a famed British architect. He designed fifty-three churches in London and many secular buildings as well.

Wren started his academic career studying astronomy and later psychology. His accomplishments in science led him to become president of the Royal Society, the oldest national scientific society in the world. At the time, the Royal Society strongly promoted scientific inquiry in various fields, and Wren wanted to bring this level of inquiry to the stagnant field of architecture. So, in 1662, he began to design the Sheldonian Theatre at Oxford. It used a classical design inspired by an ancient Roman theater, but it also integrated modern timber trusses for the roof. The theater was a gift to Oxford from Bishop Gilbert Sheldon, and while Wren was working on it, Sheldon was also discussing with Wren the rehabilitation of the dilapidated St. Paul's Cathedral in London.

Inspired by French architecture of the time, including the Palace of Versailles, the Louvre, and the domed churches of the Val-de-Grâce and the Sorbonne, in 1666 Wren created his first design for St. Paul's dome. Just a week later, though, St. Paul's Cathedral burned to the ground in the Great Fire of London, which destroyed two-thirds of the city. Wren switched his focus to planning out the rebuilding of London for Charles II. He created a plan inspired by Versailles and Rome, but his plan was never adopted. Instead, London was rebuilt as it was before the fire, only with certain streets widened and new construction standards implemented.

In 1670, funds became available for some rebuilding in London, but Wren was not involved in it, as he was now the king's surveyor and worked on royal projects. He did, however,

Construction on Sir Christopher Wren's dome for St. Paul's Cathedral in London took an astonishing thirty-five years!

contribute to the designs when fifty-two churches were rebuilt after the fire (which had destroyed eighty-seven churches). A few drawings for these rebuildings were Wren's, but many he delegated to other architects and simply oversaw and approved.

However, Wren was still working on the design for St. Paul's Cathedral. His design was approved by King Charles II, but as the old cathedral was demolished and construction was set to begin, some critics deemed Wren's design too modest. So, Wren designed a much grander model, which still didn't meet the approval of critics, who found it too spectacular. In 1675, Wren submitted yet another design, which was finally accepted, and then building started.

The first service was held in the rebuilt St. Paul's Cathedral in 1697; however, the dome was still not complete after twenty-two years of construction. The government, frustrated with the slow construction, withheld half of Wren's salary until the cathedral was completed, which finally occurred in 1711, when Wren was seventy-nine years old. In all, construction took thirty-five years. However, St. Paul's remains probably Wren's best-known work and is visited by thousands every day.

Perhaps part of why construction of St. Paul's took so long is that while he was overseeing it, Wren was still the chief architect on the city's other fifty-two churches that were being rebuilt, as well as surveyor of the king's works. Also during this time, the master of Trinity College at Cambridge University commissioned Wren to design a new library. And the dean of Christ Church at Oxford also commissioned Wren to complete the design of the main gateway to the college. Further, he was chief architect to William of Orange, who, along with his wife, Mary II, was a prolific builder. Under William and Mary, Wren designed and reconstructed Kensington Palace and Hampton Court Palace, which was a huge undertaking. In other words, Wren still had his day job!

What is amazing about Wren's work is the range of styles his work shows inspiration from. He was a master at combining classical elements with modern, forward-thinking designs. Over the years, he drew inspiration from classic European architectural styles, such as Gothicism, but designed buildings that stylistically were ahead of their time. The library Wren designed for Trinity College, for example, was designed and built when Baroque was the predominant style, but it looks more like a Neoclassical building—even though Neoclassicism wasn't to be the prevailing style for another century! No doubt, Wren's influence on architecture as a combination of art and science cannot be ignored.

be helpful, since you'll need to take classes in computer-aided design and drafting (CADD) in your bachelor's or master's degree program. In addition, business courses can also be helpful.

If you're interested in a career in architecture, consider going to a summer architecture camp while you're in high school. Various schools of architecture offer these camps for high school students to explore the field. Architecture camps are offered by the University of Notre Dame in Indiana, Illinois Institute of Technology in Chicago, and Boston Architectural College, among others. Also, Frank Lloyd Wright's Taliesin in Wisconsin offers a summer youth program.

Required Education and Training

The education and training required to become a practicing architect is not for the faint of heart. School programs and training programs are rigorous and take a lot of dedication; however, they are fun and rewarding to those who love the field.

Education

Secondary education is a requirement for a career in architecture. You can't simply become an architect out of high school, even with on-the-job training. At very least, you need a bachelor's degree in architecture, however a master's degree is preferred. In almost all states, you must earn the degree from a school accredited by the National Architectural Accrediting Board (NAAB) in the United States or the Canadian Architectural Certification Board (CACB) in Canada.

Nicknamed "the Gherkin," this modern commercial skyscraper located in London stands in stark contrast to a more traditional stone building.

For a bachelor's degree in architecture, you should expect to spend about five years on your studies. For a master's degree, you'll spend another two to five years in school (depending on whether your undergraduate degree was in architecture, too). In either degree program, you'll take courses on architectural theory and history, CADD, environmental design, structural analysis, building technology, and materials construction. You may also take classes in calculus, physics, and urban studies.

Although online study in general is becoming increasingly common, this is not really the case in architecture; the reason being because all architecture programs require you to put in time in a design studio. There you meet with other students and designated faculty to work on hands-on building projects. This is not to say that *no* architecture classes are available online; some are, but you cannot currently earn a degree in architecture through an online program alone.

Finding the best school of architecture is a very personal decision that relies on a number of factors. There is no single "best" architecture school for everyone. However, there are a number of well-regarded architectural schools that you can investigate to determine which one is best for you based on such factors as location, price, courses offered, faculty, and alumni.

According to *DesignIntelligence*, the Design Futures Council's bimonthly report, which ranks the most successful architectural schools each year, top bachelor's degree programs in architecture include Cornell University in Ithaca, New York; Cal Poly in San Luis Obispo, California; Rice University in Houston, Texas; Virginia Polytechnic Institute in Blacksburg, Virginia; Syracuse University in Syracuse, New York; University of Texas at Austin in Austin, Texas; Rhode Island School of Design in Providence, Rhode Island; Southern California Institute of Architecture in Los Angeles, California; Pratt Institute in Brooklyn, New York; and University of Southern California in Los Angeles, California.

Also according to *DesignIntelligence*, the most successful programs for a master's degree in architecture include Cornell University; Rice University; Harvard University in Cambridge, Massachusetts; Columbia University in New York, New York; Yale University in New Haven, Connecticut; MIT in Cambridge, Massachusetts; University of Michigan in Ann Arbor, Michigan; University of Pennsylvania in Philadelphia, Pennsylvania; University of Virginia in Charlottesville, Virginia; Washington University in St. Louis, Missouri; and University of California at Berkeley in Berkeley, California.

Training

In addition to the educational requirements, aspiring architects in almost every state must complete an Intern Development Program (IDP), which is facilitated by the National Council of Architectural Registration Boards (NCARB)—a federation of architectural licensing boards in each of the United States, the District of Columbia, Guam, Puerto Rico, and the US Virgin Islands. The IDP will require you to complete 5,600 training hours, which you can start earning once you have finished high school or earned your GED. This training generally must be completed under the supervision of licensed architects; however, some areas of the IDP can be completed under the supervision of a registered engineer. In general, you will be paid for the time you spend on your IDP; unpaid internships usually do not count toward your IDP. The NCARB and AIA developed the IDP in the 1970s, and the NCARB currently administers the program. The IDP allows you to experience the day-to-day responsibilities of being an architect to acquire experience in the field, explore specialized areas, and refine your ultimate career goals. The IDP is made up of four experience categories: pre-design, design, project management, and practice management. These four categories are made up of seventeen experience areas. Together, these experience

The Gothic design of Westminster Abbey looms in London, right near the River Thames.

areas help you earn the required 3,740 core minimum hours. The remaining 1,860 required hours can be from elective areas.

To document your IDP, you must register with NCARB. When you do, you will be assigned an IDP supervisor who oversees your program on a daily basis. You'll also have the opportunity to choose a mentor, who acts as an advisor or coach and whom you can consult whenever you need insight on your career. In a way, the IDP combined with a mentor is similar to the apprenticeships architects completed in the days before licensing requirements, when an aspiring architect worked under an experienced professional to learn the trade. In some cases, you can count continuing education credit and/or certification programs, such as the CSI Construction Documents Technologist (CDT) certification, toward fulfilling your IDP.

Required Exams

Up until the late 1800s, there were no licensing exams for architects. However, in 1897, Illinois became the first state to adopt a licensing law for architects, and other states followed over the next half-century. Nowadays, all fifty states require aspiring architects to pass a licensing exam before they can practice.

Once you have earned a degree in architecture and completed an IDP, you are eligible to take your state's licensing exam. In each state, the exam is called the Architect Registration Examination (ARE), and it is administered by the NCARB—the same entity with whom you register your IDP. In most states, you must complete your IDP before you take your ARE, but in some states you can take the exam while you're still working on your IDP.

The ARE is a rigorous test that includes seven different subject tests, all timed. The subject tests include programming, planning, and practice; site planning and design; building design and construction systems; schematic design; structural systems; building systems; and construction documents and services. The tests may include multiple-choice, fill-in, and illustrative questions. A few states require tests beyond the ARE for licensing, but for most states passing the ARE is sufficient.

Passing the ARE doesn't mean that your license lasts forever, though. In most states, architects have to renew their license every two years, and they must complete a certain number of continuing education credits to do so.

BEING YOUR OWN BOSS

Once you become an architect, you can go to work for an architectural firm. However, there's another option: you can start your own firm and be your own boss. Starting your own business is exciting, but it's also a big undertaking. To successfully start your own architectural firm, you need a lot of design experience, but you also need to understand the business end of the field—marketing, sales, and dealing with clients. In addition, you need to have the self-confidence to make it as an entrepreneur; you have to believe in yourself in order for your clients to believe in you; and you need to have the confidence in your firm and your ability to withstand the lean times while you wait for the prosperous times. To be successful as an independent architect, you also need to know the market and know where to find clients. Is there a market for your firm? If you specialize in designing barns and you hope to set up a firm in Manhattan, chances are there won't be much market for your design skills. And chances are, you won't find many prospective clients since Manhattan isn't exactly known as a farming community!

These are the types of things you need to look at when you're considering whether to join (or stay with) a firm or whether to strike out on your own. Analyze the market and your skill set, and see whether an independent operation is right for you.

Additional Requirements

In some states, you need to complete only the education (accredited bachelor's or master's program), experience (via your IDP), and examination (your ARE) to call yourself an architect. However, some states have additional requirements you must fulfill to begin practicing as an architect. When you get to that point, the NCARB will help you find out what other requirements your state may have.

There's no doubt that becoming an architect requires a lot of education and even more hard work. However, if you're interested in design, the career is well worth the effort. In the next chapter, we'll look at a day in the life of an architect.

An architect's typical day is rich and varied, with time spent at jobsites, with clients, and behind the desk.

CHAPTER 3

On the Job

Being an architect sounds like a glamorous job! You get to sit and sketch out design ideas all day, and hopefully at some point you'll design the next Golden Gate Bridge or Sydney Opera House—a structure that will remind people of your name for years to come! What could be more exciting than that? Answer: paperwork. Lots of paperwork. Just kidding; paperwork isn't overly exciting, but it is part of an architect's job, so you might as well embrace the tedious with the glamorous.

What Exactly Does an Architect Do?

There's a lot involved in being an architect—possibly more than you expected. First, architects have to meet with clients to determine a given project's objectives and requirements. For example, if the architect designs custom homes, he or she must meet with the homeowners to find out what features they want the home to have and what the local permitting requirements are for such a home. If the home is in a protected landscape area, for example, there may be extremely strict requirements related to building new structures. Architects need to know these requirements and work with clients to design a structure that fits within them.

Working with design plans and blueprints is just one of an architect's many tasks.

Once an architect and a client have a design concept in mind, the architect must prepare estimates for the project, including amounts of required materials, equipment needed for the building process, construction time required, and, of course, the costs associated with all of these factors. Next, the architect must prepare the specifications for the structure and design the construction plans. These plans show the building's appearance and important construction details, but they also must include plans for the structural system, **HVAC** system, electrical and communications systems, plumbing system, and perhaps even landscape plans. The architect may prepare these plans independently but usually works with other professionals, such as architectural engineers, who specialize in certain areas— for example, the architect may work with an architectural engineer to design the building's electrical system. These plans may be hand-drawn, but it's much more likely that the architect creates them using CADD software or building information modeling.

Once all plans have been approved and all necessary permits obtained, construction can begin. At that point, the architect likely visits the building site to ensure the contractors are working per the design and on schedule, producing quality results. Some architects will help clients

Architects visit jobsites to ensure that projects are running smoothly.

get construction bids and choose contracts, and they may even help clients negotiate construction contracts.

A Day in the Life

So what does a day in the life of an architect look like? If you've imagined that an architect sits at a drafting table all day creating amazing sketches of proposed buildings, you'd be incorrect. Architects *do* create amazing sketches and computer-aided drawings of proposed buildings, but they do a lot more, too.

It's hard to describe a typical day in the life of an architect because what they do varies by the day and by the project, but let's look at a common scenario.

You might start your day by swinging by the jobsite. Once a building is under construction, the construction crew is handling a lot of the day-to-day tasks that come with actually *building* the structure. However, the architect still needs to regularly visit the jobsite to ensure that tasks are being completed correctly, on budget, and on schedule. Some architects refer to this part of their job as construction administration—essentially, overseeing the actual construction of the project.

From there, you might head to a client meeting. Architects have to meet with clients to discuss what they want to see in their project, but these meetings are also beneficial for the architect. Suppose an architect builds custom single-family homes. Hearing what clients want is important for each client's specific house, but it also gives the architect a good feel for what clients in general are looking for in terms of style and design. In other words, what the architect learns from his or her clients can inform future designs for other clients. Keep in mind that you often have to be sales savvy as an architect. Your potential clients are poised to spend a *lot* of money, and you want to convince them why they should do so with your firm

Frank Lloyd Wright: Prairie Architect (June 8, 1867–April 9, 1959)

Frank Lloyd Wright was born Frank Lincoln Wright in Richland Center, Wisconsin, in 1867. He may be the best-known American architect to date. He is the designer behind the **Prairie style**, which was the basis for residential building design in the United States in the twentieth century.

Wright developed the Prairie style of architecture, which described low-lying houses built in the Midwest, in the early 1900s. These houses were usually two stories with a single-

Frank Lloyd Wright is responsible for the Prairie style of architecture, prominent in the Midwest in the early twentieth century.

story wing. They featured horizontal lines, gently sloped roofs, ribbon windows that frequently wrapped around corners, suppressed chimneys, overhangs, and sequestered gardens. The interiors of Prairie-style homes featured bold, plain walls and roomy, open living spaces. They were built using mass-produced materials and equipment that was otherwise generally used for commercial building development.

By the early 1900s, Wright was also building apartments, group dwellings, recreation centers, and even churches. His Unity Temple for the Unitarian Church of Oak Park, Illinois, constructed in the early 1900s, was registered as a national historic landmark in 1971. Today, the church congregation still meets in Wright's historic building.

After spending some time writing books in Europe, Wright returned to the United States and, in 1912, designed his first skyscraper, which was never built. In 1912 and 1913, Wright spent some time in Japan and some time in Chicago, working on the construction of Midway Gardens, which was artistically abstract and eye-catching but was demolished after it failed due to **Prohibition.**

In 1929, Wright designed what some consider to be his best concept: a tower of studios **cantilevered** from a concrete core. He intended it to be built in New York City, but that never happened. Instead, it was built in 1956 as the Price Tower in Bartlesville, Oklahoma.

However, the great stock market crash of 1929 and the onset of the Great Depression halted all architectural activity, so Wright began giving lectures in Chicago, New York City, and in New Jersey at Princeton University. He also established the Taliesin Fellowship, which was a training program for architects and artists. This program attracted twenty to sixty apprentices each year. In the winter, the crew went to Arizona, where they

Wright's Taliesin North is located in Spring Green, Wisconsin.

were working on Taliesin West. At the same time, Wright was developing a successful system for building low-cost homes. These weren't Prairie houses; instead, they were flat-roofed single-story homes on a heated concrete foundation mat, and they were called Usonians.

Wright gradually earned back his reputation, and as the economy improved, he went on to build Fallingwater near Pittsburgh, Pennsylvania. The house was cantilevered over a waterfall so that it almost appears to be floating over the water. It is now a popular tourist attraction. Around this same time, he also designed and built the administrative center for S.C. Johnson Wax in Racine, Wisconsin, which is regarded as one of the most humane workrooms in modern architecture, with its airy openness and top-lit space.

instead of another. You're not a salesperson per se, but you need to be able to "sell" your firm.

After the morning's meetings are out of the way, you might head to your office to get to work. Only, as in many other white-collar professions, you may find that responding to e-mail and phone calls takes up *way* too much of your time! Keep in mind that architects are often the coordinator for a project, so their job can include managing all of the subcontractors and other people working on a project. The architect needs to keep everyone on the team informed about the building progress but also needs to hire people to join the team when necessary. So on a typical day, you might spend time interviewing people to work on a project, or you might spend time updating those people you've already hired on how the project is going relative to scope and budget.

Oh, and wait! There are permits to deal with—always permits. As an architect, you have to make sure that your projects meet current building codes and zoning laws, and you have to make sure to obtain the proper permits. Even if someone else on the team does the drudgework of filing for the permit, you still have to make sure the permit is actually granted. Work on a project cannot start until the appropriate permits are in place.

At some point during the day, you'll have to eat lunch, because everyone eats lunch. And like everyone in the working world, you'll have to find time to nourish yourself! However, before you do that, you need to prepare the project budget for the client you met with two days ago. You promised the client she'd have the budget by the end of today, and now it's looking like the permits may cost more than you originally estimated. Uh-oh. And before you can finish the budget, your colleague stops by to remind you that you need to coordinate the environmental impact study that needs to be done for another site. Just one more thing on your to-do list.

Next, you might start working on preliminary sketches for a new project you hope to do for a client and you might find time to revise the sketches you did for another client, who wasn't happy with the preliminary sketches. Back to the drawing board, as they say …

As in almost any job, you'll likely have to play "firefighter," addressing unexpected problems that crop up and putting out "fires." Contractors aren't infallible, and you'll undoubtedly run into situations where someone hasn't done something correctly, and now you have to handle the problem. It's stressful, but it's life … and it happens in almost any profession.

Specializations in the Field

When we think of architects, we usually think of the people who design buildings or bridges. However, there are specializations in the field of architecture, including landscape architects; naval architects; architectural engineers; architectural drafters; and architectural historians; and, of course, there are professors needed to teach in all of these fields, so interested people in the field may eventually choose a career in academia.

Landscape Architects

Instead of designing buildings, landscape architects design land areas, such as parks, recreational facilities, school campuses, and other open spaces. Much like an architect who designs buildings and other structures, an aspiring landscape architect must earn a degree from an accredited university, gain internship experience, and pass an exam (the Landscape Architect Registration Exam).

Landscape architects must work in conjunction with clients, engineers, and building architects to design the space for their common project. The landscape architect then prepares a site plan and cost estimate. The site plan is generally created using CADD software and shows graphic representations of the landscape features, along with any proposed structures. Landscape architects must be intimately familiar with the environment in which they are working and must consider land conditions when designing a plan. For example, a landscape architect in a desert climate would most likely choose drought-tolerant plants that are native to the desert rather than trees and shrubs that thrive in a moist, cool climate.

Like building architecture, landscape architecture is an art and a science. The landscape architect considers environmental conditions and concerns when creating a design but also keeps in mind the aesthetics of the area and tries to enhance its natural beauty. Landscape architects are also pivotal in **environmental conservation**, as they help preserve and restore historic landscapes.

Naval Architects

It's probably not surprising to learn that naval architects design and build ships! These can be as simple as sailboats to as complex as aircraft carriers and submarines. The naval architect works on the basic design of the vessel, considering form and stability, and a marine engineer works on the mechanical systems involved. The two collaborate to design the boiler room, HVAC system, refrigeration equipment, and propulsion machinery.

Naval architects focus heavily on the craft's hull, designing sectional and waterline curves to establish a

GOOD WORKS: EMERGENCY FLOOR

Two recent graduates from Rice University's School of Architecture, Scott Austin Key and Sam Brisendine, are focused on using their knowledge of architecture and building to give back and improve the world where they can. Their brainchild, Emergency Floor, was conceived when they considered the plight of refugees who were forced to sleep on the ground in shelters. Sleeping on the dirt leaves refugees fleeing from war, conflict, or natural disasters vulnerable to not only extreme cold in some climates but also to parasitic infections and disease.

Coming together to form Good Works Studio, the two men created Emergency Floor out of a waste product commonly found at refugee camps: shipping pallets. The discarded pallets are plentiful at many refugee camps, and Key and Brisendine's modular, plastic coverings slide over and snap onto the pallets. Then the plastic-covered pallets can be placed, like pieces of a puzzle, to fit any kind of shelter.

In addition to solving the problem of people sleeping on the ground in unsanitary conditions, Emergency Floor helps reduce waste by reusing the shipping pallets, and it's economically feasible because it reuses a waste product. Emergency Floor can be produced for as little as $2 per square foot, which makes the cost reasonable for humanitarian organizations that aid refugees.

Good Works Studio is a small venture, and Key and Brisendine are new to the field, but they didn't let a little thing like that discourage them. To qualify for a USAID grant that would allow them to get Emergency Floor into an initial ten refugee shelters in Iraq and Nepal, Key and Brisendine took to social media and launched an Indiegogo campaign to raise enough funds to qualify for USAID's Development Innovation Ventures (DIV) grant. They used the power of social media and a relevant hashtag to encourage people to #getofftheground and show their support. They not only raised enough money to qualify for the grant; they also attracted the attention of the Design Futures Council, who named them Emerging Leaders of 2015!

Good Works and Emergency Floor are good reminders that the sky really can be the limit. No matter how modest your operation or your goals, with a little creativity you can accomplish your objectives. For Key and Brisendine, those goals were simple: "No one should have to sleep in the dirt. We believe in the power of design to innovate; we believe we should be actively working to make the world a better place." With a little help from their friends, USAID, and the power of social media, Key and Brisendine's dream will become a reality, and thousands of refugees will be able to #getofftheground.

center of gravity for the ship and to ensure buoyancy and stability. They also design the ship's interior, such as cargo spaces, passenger compartments, elevators, and common areas. Naval architects also evaluate ship performance in trials to ensure optimal performance and that the craft meets national and international standards.

An aspiring naval architect must earn a degree from an accredited program. They generally must take an exam for a mariner's license from the US Coast Guard, too.

Architectural Engineers

Architectural engineers, also known as civil engineers, perform some similar tasks to architects, but the careers have a different focus. An architect focuses on the building design as it relates to aesthetics and function, whereas an architectural engineer focuses on support systems for the building and its operation.

Architectural engineers work on buildings, roads, bridges, airports, and tunnels, among other structures. They analyze data such as maps and reports to determine the necessary underlying structure needed for a project. They are intimately familiar with government regulations and permitting, and they often compile and submit the necessary permits for a project, as well as identify potential environmental hazards of a project. They perform soil testing to determine whether the land underneath a proposed structure can support it, and they also test building materials that will be used in various projects.

Like architects, architectural engineers provide cost and materials estimates and use design software to create plans for proposed structures or transportation systems. Unlike architects, architectural engineers don't necessarily always meet with the client to discuss design; however, architectural engineers do present their findings about a proposed building's structure and impact to the public. They also perform or oversee surveying operations, which allows them to establish grades, elevations, and reference points for the building construction.

Like architects, architectural engineers must earn a degree from an accredited program, and they must pass appropriate licensing exams.

Architectural Drafters

Architectural drafters, also known as CADD operators or simply drafters, use CADD software to create technical drawings based on the designs of architects. They work under the supervision of architects and create drawings based on the architect's specifications and rough designs. They also sometimes add details to the plans based on their knowledge of building techniques. Architectural drafters also specify dimensions and materials for a building project, and also provide direction on how to build it.

Architectural drafters must be expert CADD users so they can create plans that can be put into building information modeling systems and product data management systems. This way, drafters can work together with architects, construction managers, and engineers on the digital models of a project.

Some architectural drafters specialize in a particular area, such as residential buildings or commercial buildings, or by material used, such as steel, wood, or concrete. Like architects, architectural drafters must complete a program of study beyond a high school diploma or equivalent. However, the drafting program is a bit shorter than the bachelor's or master's degree in architecture; drafters simply need a two-year associate's degree in drafting from a community college or technical school.

Unlike architects, architectural drafters aren't required to be certified. However, certification generally helps architectural drafters demonstrate their competence in the field and can help with job prospects. Drafters can become certified by passing the American Design Drafting Association's certification.

Architectural Historian

Architectural historians are experts in the history of architecture. They help record and preserve historic structures. Their research helps determine whether a particular structure should be designated a national or state historic property. Once a building receives this designation, it is protected from being demolished in the interest of newer development. (This isn't to say a historic property is *never* demolished—one deemed hazardous may be, but a designated historic property can't be demolished simply for the purposes of building, say, a new shopping mall.)

Architectural historians study architectural history so that they are extremely familiar with architectural features of a given region or era. When deciding whether a property should be classified as historic, they look at the neighborhood surrounding the structure and the structure's significance to the community, along with architectural details and style.

Architectural historians often work in academia, teaching at colleges and universities, but they may also work for government agencies, museums, and archival centers. Some even work as freelance consultants.

Which to Choose?

You know you want to build things, but with so many specializations and career options available in the field of architecture, which should you choose? First, consider your interests. There are three main types of architects, as mentioned earlier: building architects, landscape architects, and naval architects. Ask yourself: What do you most enjoy building? Do you see yourself constructing skyscrapers? Office parks? Sports stadiums? Single-family homes? Apartment buildings? For any of those, you'll likely want to go the route of a building architect. But what if you prefer to be outside? Do you instead see yourself creating beautiful parks and public spaces that people will enjoy for years to come? Do you have an interest in the environment and in working with local natural resources? If so, then you might want to consider becoming a landscape architect. If ships and the sea are passions for you, then perhaps you want to build aquatic vessels. Becoming a naval architect will allow you to combine your interests in building and maritime life.

Second, consider what you want to do with your days. Do you want to talk directly to clients to help them create something that realizes their dream? If so, then you definitely want to be an architect—either building, landscape, or naval. However, if you're the type of person who shudders at the thought of having a lot of client contact, then you might rather invest your time and energy into becoming an architectural engineer. That way, you're still intricately involved in the building process (in whatever area you choose), but you're also rarely required to talk to clients. Instead, you're working closely with the architect and the contractors to manage certain aspects of the building process. Or, if you feel like teaching is your calling, consider becoming an architectural historian.

Think, too, about the time you want to devote to schooling and certification. Becoming an architect or an architectural engineer requires rigorous postsecondary education, internships, and examinations, and becoming an architectural historian usually requires a master's degree, and sometimes even a PhD. If that sounds about as appealing as a root canal, then consider becoming an architectural drafter. The school commitment is much less demanding, and you don't necessarily have to become certified.

Whatever path you choose, you're in for a fun ride. Being a part of a team that creates something is an exciting adventure—whether that something is a building, a house, a ship, or a beautiful park. You'll get to work hard to contribute to a tangible end product, which should bring you an enormous sense of satisfaction every time you complete a project.

The Frank Gehry-designed Beekman Tower in New York City.

CHAPTER 4

The Future

No matter what career you're interested in, it's important to consider the long term. When you enter the working world, is it likely you'll be able to find work in your chosen field? Will that field pay a living wage? Will you have to relocate? No one has a crystal ball to provide a look into the future, but you can take a look at expert predictions and get a fairly good idea of the outlook for your chosen career.

Career Outlook

When you're considering your future career, one of the most important things to look at is the projected job outlook. Another important piece is the salary, although in the long term, some people are willing to settle for a smaller salary if it means working at a job they truly enjoy.

Job Prospects

According to the Bureau of Labor Statistics' (BLS) *Occupational Outlook Handbook*, the job outlook for building architects is better than average. Projected change in employment from 2012 to 2022 for *all* occupations in the United States is 11 percent. The projected growth for building architects, on the other hand, is a robust 17 percent! The outlook isn't quite as good for naval architects—the projected job growth for the same time period is 10 percent. But if it's landscape architecture you're interested in, you'll fall right in the middle, with a projected job growth of 14 percent—which, remember, is still above the overall projected job growth for all occupations.

The BLS notes that school districts and universities are expected to need architects in the coming years, as school buildings age. Also, architects will be needed to design more health care facilities as the **Baby Boomer** generation ages and begins to require more options.

Further, the environment is driving the need for architects with a background in **sustainable design**, which uses resources as efficiently as possible and with as little impact on the environment as possible. The BLS suggests that architects with skill areas in sustainable design may have a competitive advantage in the coming years.

Green roofs add beauty to Monte Carlo in Monaco.

The same holds true for landscape architects. With the heavy focus on environmental consciousness and the increased demands for sustainability, landscape architects will be in demand to redesign public and private spaces. Green roofs, which are covered in vegetation and can reduce air and water pollution as well as heating and cooling costs, are becoming more common, and landscape architects with knowledge of how to design them will be in greater demand. Similarly, with increased interest in conserving storm-water runoff and avoiding the potential pollution of waterways, landscape architects will continue to be in demand.

Another area with some expected growth is naval architecture. Naval architects design and modify cargo ships, specifically those that transport energy products such as liquefied natural gas. There are new emissions and pollution regulations on these vessels, so naval architects will be needed to help modify existing ships and build new ones.

In any of the architecture fields, strong technical knowledge, communication skills, and knowledge of environmental and/or building codes and regulations are prized and will help you gain a competitive edge.

Salary

Salary is certainly an important piece of any career you're considering. How important a piece is really up to you. Some people want to make a lot of money, and others are content to make less if it means that they can do a job they truly enjoy. After all, there's a reason people choose to be teachers, and it isn't the pay! The same holds true for a number of other notoriously low-paying jobs.

The good news is if you want to be an architect, you don't need to worry much about salary. It's not fantastically high paying—you're not necessarily going to pull in the multi-millions of a sports professional or a rock star, for example. However, it's a decently paying profession where you can make a good living.

According to the BLS, the median annual wage for building architects in 2012 was almost $74,000. The lowest-paid 10 percent of architects in the field made just over $44,000 annually, and the highest-paid 10 percent made more than $118,000 annually. To provide a comparison, the median annual wage for *all* occupations in the United States in 2012 was just under $35,000. Do the math, and you can see that the median annual wage for architects is double that—which is not too shabby!

Whether you receive benefits in addition to your salary depends entirely on the firm and your position. If you're a self-employed architect, you'll have to pay for your medical benefits yourself. The same likely holds true if you're a contractor. If you're a full-time employee of a firm, though, you'll likely receive some sort of benefits package as part of your overall compensation. As a bonus, some firms will pay the tuition and fees to cover your continuing education requirements when you need to renew your license.

The median annual wage for landscape architects in 2012 was a bit lower, at just above $64,000. However, that's still almost double the median annual wage for *all* occupations in the United States, so again not too shabby!

You want to go where the money *really* is? Then be a naval architect, for whom the median annual salary is just over $88,000. That's two and a half times the median annual salary for all occupations! And the top 10 percent of naval architects in 2012 made approximately $150,000 per year.

So what's the catch? Well, remember, job growth is projected to be slower for naval architects than for building architects and landscape architects. The number of jobs is smaller, too—in 2022, only 8,100 jobs are expected to be available for naval architects, whereas there are expected to be 126,000 jobs for building architects and 22,900 for landscape architects. So be sure to factor that into your thoughts about the future: there's a much smaller playing field for naval architects than for building architects and even landscape architects, but if you can get onto the playing field, it's a pretty good place to be, salary-wise.

One thing to keep in mind about salary is that it's largely dependent on where you live. Certain areas of the country are much more expensive than others. The San Francisco Bay Area, for example, is one of the most expensive places to live in the continental United States, and wages reflect that. According to salary website Glassdoor.com, the average salary of an architect in San Francisco in 2015 was $103,226 per year, but according to Salary.com, architects in Omaha, Nebraska, made a median annual wage of only $76,451. That's a big difference in wages—but there's also a big difference in cost of living between San Francisco and Omaha!

Pros and Cons of a Career in Architecture

Becoming an architect is not for the faint of heart. It's a very rewarding job, but there are also a lot of challenges in it. The schooling, for example, is rigorous. Good architecture programs are *extremely* competitive, and if you're fortunate enough to get accepted into one, you'll likely find yourself surrounded by Type A personalities who are driven to succeed. If you want to last in your program, you'll have to work extremely hard to keep up. College won't be an endless round of parties for you; however, you'll undoubtedly come to enjoy the company of your would-be architect friends who have a similar end goal to yours.

Besides the program being rigorous, it's rather long. You can expect to spend at least five years earning a degree in architecture, and more if you decide to earn your master's degree. That's a lot of schooling, and schooling doesn't come cheap! On the flip side, once you receive your degree and begin working in the field, you will likely make a pretty decent salary.

Othon Benavente is an architect at Studio Benavente Architects, Inc., in the greater San Francisco Bay Area, which specializes in commercial interiors in Class A offices. A graduate of UC Berkeley, he has worked in the industry for almost thirty-nine years. Over those years, he has assembled a portfolio of residential, corporate, restaurant, commercial office, airport, hotel, theme park, and industrial projects for a variety of firms, large and small. He has owned and managed his own firm of architect interns and interior designers for the past twenty-three years.

What do you enjoy most about being an architect?

There's a lot of personal expression. You can really carve out your own world; you create your own reality. There's an aspect of it that's just fun.

We specialize in commercial interiors in Class A office buildings. It's very fast paced. What I enjoy most is the conceptual aspect. When you design an office, you design it with a vision as to the head of the office, the body of the office, the flow, the function. You develop an overall concept that drives the solution. It's not about opinion, it's not about what you or I like, or who has better taste; it's driven by a concept, and the concept will determine whether it is right or not. It doesn't matter whether it's a thousand square feet (93 square meters) or 350,000 square feet (32,516 sq m); you have to have a concept. And when you think that way, you begin to see patterns. It's not linear; it's proportional and intuitive.

When I start sketching, amid all the scribbles, I begin to discern patterns. Within those patterns are cadences and rhythms. Every building has sorts of frequencies. There's column spacing; there's window spacing. When you first look at a plan, it may not be immediately obvious, but it was originally laid out on a grid. Once you have that grid, it may be irregular and you may deviate from it, but there's a pattern and a rhythm. Once you determine what that pattern is, you find the cadence. It's almost like a song. It's really satisfying.

What is your *least* favorite part of the job?

There are lots and lots of parameters. Lots of times people like a plan and wonder why you did something, but the plan is derived after studying building codes and fire codes and construction technologies. There's a series of things to consider, and you have to jump through hoops to meet requirements. You have to calculate the occupant load and determine how many exits you have to leave out of the space. You have to determine the separation between the exits. You have to research a bunch of stuff relative to the code, but you also have to know how the local building official is going to interpret the code. There are so many gray areas that it's hard to know what's right. The building inspector will have one interpretation, the fire inspector will have another, the field inspector will have another …

Everybody has an agenda, and even when you're working a design, you have to thread a needle through lots of people's agendas to find what works. If you're skilled, you're able to drive the process and really let the original concept drive the solution. It's not linear; it's an iterative process. You try this and it works and gets vetoed by one authority, and you try that and it works and gets vetoed by another … and you go back and forth. The simplest plan can take a long time. In fact, the smaller the plan, the longer it takes to resolve because you're trying to reconcile so many things within a small space.

CHAT WITH AN ARCHITECT: OTHON BENAVENTE

An architect has to not only resolve the problem, but he also needs to lead—you've got engineers, you've got contractors, you've got subcontractors who know their particular specialty better than you, and they may make changes without telling you. And then you go back and say, "That's not what I intended; that's not how I designed it," but it's too late. You're sort of like the conductor, but the musicians are getting direction from lots of different sources. You've got to understand people's agendas; you've got to be a people person.

The other thing that's frustrating is the structure of the profession. When you're looking at the medical profession, doctors have organized themselves in such a way that they do what they like to do, and they delegate to nurses and EMTs things that they don't like to do. There is an [organizational] chart of all these functions in the medical profession that are handled by other people all the way down the line. Then you look at the legal profession and it's the same thing—there are all these functions that are delegated down the line to paralegals and legal secretaries, leaving the attorney with the things he likes to do.

But as for an architect, the profession is not as well structured. In most firms, the way an architect advances is that he stops doing what he loves to do, and he begins to push paper. You get to do what you love to do less, and you delegate to other people to do the things you thought you'd be doing for the rest of your life.

What made you want to be an architect?

It never crossed my mind, actually. I was actually a psych major, and then I remember someone asking me what I was studying, and she told me I'd never get a job or make any money in psychology. I got discouraged, and a counselor told me to take a Strong Interest Inventory. That test doesn't test what you're *good* at; it tests your interests. And it came up with architecture. Up until that point, it hadn't even crossed my mind. I didn't draw; I didn't do anything like that. When that test came up with architecture and I said, "Yeah, I'm going to do that," I remember my counselor chasing me down the hall and saying, "That test doesn't mean you *can* do this!" But I did, and I became good at drawing, and I found I really loved it. I loved the theory, I loved the philosophy … I just got consumed by the study of it. And when I realized the whole ambience of it, I loved it. It's all about travel and history, and I don't know how I could've missed that. So that's how I kind of fell into it.

Any advice you'd give to young people interested in pursuing a career in architecture?

It's really exciting. I mean, it's very demanding—the study is very hard, the schools are impacted. You work like a fiend, and you feel like you're about two inches tall sometimes. You've got egomaniacal professors trashing your work in public. You come out into the field, and it's not really well compensated. There are a lot of demands, a lot of deadlines. It's feast or famine, and layoffs are part of the industry.

But there's an aspect of it that is a vocation you do because you love to do it. It's not a function of the money; it's something you were born to do. It's really a satisfying profession.

Then there's the job itself. As mentioned in Chapter 3, being an architect doesn't mean sitting at a drafting table and sketching ideas and concepts all day. There's a lot of paperwork and client contact involved, too. That can be a pro or a con, really. Some people detest paperwork and/or aren't terribly comfortable meeting with clients. For those people, it's obviously a con. However, the varied duties of an architect also mean that your days are full of variety, and no two days are spent the same way. Many people enjoy that type of variety in their career.

Having a career with a lot of day-to-day variety generally means that you must be good at multitasking, and that is definitely true for architects. Most practicing architects work on more than one project at a time, so they must juggle half a dozen or more different projects and devote the necessary attention to each one. To a client, his or her project should be your top priority. That's fine, but if you have six such clients, you can see where challenges might start to crop up. Maybe three of your six clients want designs on their desk by Friday. That's a tall order, but you pretty much have to fulfill it, which can mean some long working hours.

You also need to check your ego at the door when working with clients. Understandably, clients generally have strong opinions about what they want to see in their

Modern architectural designs often incorporate lots of windows to let in as much natural light as possible.

project. After all, they're spending at least hundreds of thousands of dollars on it, if not millions. But problems can arise when a client changes his or her mind about something. "But I said I wanted *square* windows, not rectangular!" the client might insist. Deep down, you know the client asked for rectangular windows—it's in the notes you took at the first client meeting, but you can't really call the client out on the change in wishes; instead, you need to adhere to that idea that the client is always right, and make it happen. It may be at increased cost to the client if you've already ordered the rectangular windows and you can't return them, but somehow, you need to make it happen and that sometimes requires checking your own ego at the door.

With all that said, though, being an architect is a rewarding, well-paying career. Despite the challenges, most architects truly enjoy their work. They love architecture, and they love being a part of the creation process. They love contributing something lasting to the landscape and seeing their ideas brought to life. In any career, you take the bad with the good, and architects generally do that and find that the pros outweigh the cons.

Tips for Getting That All-Important Internship

Internships are key in becoming an architect. They're useful in many careers, but they're especially useful in architecture because of that good old IDP requirement that you read about in Chapter 2. Landing an internship, however, can be challenging. Just as architecture schools are fiercely competitive, so are internships. If you want to earn one, here are some general tips on how to make your résumé stand out.

- **Design**. Design is part of the job of being an architect, so you want anything you submit to look well designed. Don't just use Microsoft Word's résumé template to throw together a quick résumé. Instead, spend some time focusing on the aesthetics of your résumé. It should look clean and appealing when people at the firm first glance at it.

- **Interests**. Showcase your interests on your résumé. They may not even be directly related to architecture, but they give you something to talk about with the firm—something that makes you stand out from the dozens of other résumés the firm members are looking through. Do you collect vintage baseball cards, for example? Mention that in an Interests section on your résumé. You never know when a firm member will turn out to be an avid baseball fan, and that little bit of information can make you stand out.

- **Social media**. Anyone and everyone is on social media these days—use it. Follow your favorite firms' Twitter feeds or Like their Facebook pages. That will keep you up to date on the current happenings at the firm, and if you're lucky enough to score an interview, you'll be knowledgeable enough to discuss firm specifics with the interviewers.

- **Show your face**. E-mail is easy and great, but you're still just a faceless entity. If you can find a way to get a face-to-face meeting with someone at the firm, do it. Firms have events, and firm members sometimes

Frank Gehry: Postmodern Architect (February 28, 1929–)

Frank Gehry (originally Frank Owen Goldberg) was born in Toronto, Canada, to a Polish and Jewish family. His grandfather owned a hardware store, and as a child Frank would use items he found in the store to build imaginary homes and cities.

Gehry moved to the United States at the age of twenty and worked a variety of jobs in Los Angeles while attending college. He earned a degree from the University of Southern California School of Architecture, and while there he changed his last name from Goldberg to Gehry to try to avoid **anti-Semitism**. He married Anita Snyder and enrolled at the Harvard Graduate School of Design in Boston, Massachusetts. Gehry and his wife had two daughters but later divorced, and Gehry ended up dropping out of Harvard. In 1975, he remarried and had two more children with Berta Isabel Aguilera.

After he dropped out of Harvard, Gehry went back to California and launched a cardboard furniture line called Easy Edges. Just like it sounds, this was furniture made out of **corrugated** cardboard. The furniture was sold from 1969 to 1973.

However, furniture design wasn't Gehry's real interest. He wanted to build things, as he had done with the items from his grandfather's hardware store. Only he wanted to build *real* buildings now. So, he used money he earned from Easy Edges to remodel his family's Santa Monica home. The remodel was unusual and inventive—Gehry surrounded the existing house with corrugated steel and chain link fencing, which effectively

Frank Gehry is the architect behind the striking Walt Disney Concert Hall in Los Angeles.

split the house open, and incorporated an angled skylight. It was a bold design that attracted attention in the architectural world, and he began designing more homes in the Southern California area.

Gehry became somewhat of a celebrity with his **postmodern** architecture, and soon he started designing high-concept buildings, such as the Walt Disney Concert Hall in Los Angeles; the Experience Music Project in Seattle; and the Guggenheim Museum in Bilbao, Spain. In 2011, Gehry finished his first skyscraper, in New York City, as well as the Opus Hong Kong tower in China.

Many of Gehry's designs are considered **Deconstructivist** architecture. This type of architecture breaks the rule that form must follow function and challenges traditional or typical design aesthetics. Deconstructivist architects use non-rectilinear shapes that distort the structure's appearance and make it look geometrically shocking. Several current architects work in this style, but Gehry is probably the best known.

As well as being known as a Deconstructivist, Gehry is known for using unusual materials such as corrugated metal in his designs. They give his work a crude, sometimes rough, urban feel.

In addition to designing, Gehry has been a professor of architecture at Columbia University, Yale, and the University of Southern California. He has received numerous awards and accolades, but perhaps the most prestigious is the 1989 Pritzker Prize, which honors architects whose work "has produced consistent and significant contributions to humanity."

Although Gehry is now in his eighties, he is still working. He's involved in a new Guggenheim facility in Abu Dhabi, the Facebook headquarters in California, and a Dwight D. Eisenhower monument in Washington, DC.

Although Gehry is somewhat of a celebrity who is sometimes called a "starchitect"—in 2010, *Vanity Fair* referred to him as "the most important architect of our age"—Gehry insists that he is simply an architect, saying, "There are people who design buildings that are not technically and financially good, and there are those who do. Two categories, simple." Gehry's confidence comes from the fact that few would dispute that he belongs in the latter category.

give speeches or lectures. Go to these events and get your face known. (Okay, don't be a creepy stalker, but do make it a point to at least introduce yourself to the firm members.)

- **Know the firm members**. Don't just address your résumé "To Whom It May Concern." If you do, it's likely to go right to the bottom of the pile. Google the firm and find out the partners' names; then address your résumé directly to them. It takes thirty seconds, and it makes a difference. Trust me.

- **Edit your résumé**. Do *not* turn in a résumé with spelling or mechanical errors. It screams "sloppy!" and that doesn't bode well for you. Architecture is a career based on precision, and sending in a résumé with errors in it won't give them much confidence in your precision.

- **Keep work samples small**. Firms likely won't open a large-sized file attachment if you attach some drawings you've done. Keep it small and just pick your best work—the file should be no more than a few megabytes in size.

- **Show initiative**. Have you taken extra initiative to try to start learning about architecture? If so, show the firm. Show them the 3-D model you built "just for fun." If a firm is going to invest the time in an intern, they want someone with the initiative to further his or her learning as much as possible. Show them you have that.

Job Search Tips

Naturally, an internship will be extremely beneficial to your future career in architecture. If you're lucky, perhaps you'll make a contact at your internship that will lead to a job offer for you. But what if you're *not* that lucky? What if your internship was a good experience, but it didn't lead to a job offer? Well, then you're stuck doing what most people do: embarking on the almighty job hunt.

Creating a Résumé

When it comes time to apply for jobs, you'll most certainly need a résumé. You may need one earlier than that, when you're working on getting an internship, but if you don't have one by the time you start job hunting, then now's the time.

Dozens of books have been written on how to craft a good résumé; for a detailed description of how to do so, check one out. For now, here are the highlights.

A good résumé will concisely and clearly show a potential employer who you are and why the employer should hire you. But how do you do that? How do you sum up everything important about who you are and why you're a good candidate for a job in just a sheet or two of paper? Simple: you focus on the important facts and features.

Good résumés have a number of features in common:

- **They list experience and education in reverse chronological order**. Whatever experience you have, you should list it in reverse chronological order, with the most recent experience or education at the top. Employers are most interested in what you've done recently, so don't bury it at the bottom of your résumé.

- **They include a professional phone number and e-mail address**. If an employer calls you, you don't really want your five-year-old sister picking up the phone and saying something embarrassing. Provide a number for a phone that *you* will answer. The embarrassment factor is key in e-mail addresses, too. Provide a professional-sounding e-mail address, not the JohnLovesStarWars@gmail.com address you created when you were a sixth-grade sci-fi fan. You can easily get a free e-mail address from Gmail or any one of a number of other services, so set up a professional-sounding one, such as JohnSmith@gmail.com.

- **They list achievements concisely**. You may have a lot of achievements you want to showcase, and that's great, but do it in short bullet points. Remember that employers get hundreds of résumés for any given job opening, so they tend to skim quickly through them. A short bulleted list of your awards and achievements will get the employer's attention; a long paragraph explaining every award in detail is likely to be ignored.

- **They are clean and free of mistakes**. This is a big one. Although you are applying for architectural jobs instead of writing or editing jobs, you still want to be sure your résumé is completely free of spelling and grammatical errors and inconsistencies. Nothing turns potential employers off faster than a résumé riddled with errors. It shows sloppiness and a lack of attention to detail—two characteristics that won't thrill any potential employer.

- **They use white space**. It's tempting to try to cram as much information as possible in the one or two allotted pages for a résumé, but try to refrain from doing so. Résumés that use white space are easier to read and less likely to get tossed aside when the reader gets frustrated with trying to pore through dense blocks of text.

- **They use simple fonts and no color.** Simplicity is key in résumés. Using colors and fancy fonts tend to make them cluttered and distracting to read. It's best to stick to black and white and use a simple font. On a related note, skip using images in résumés. They may look a little boring as text-only, but that really is preferred.

- **They are available in a universally accessible format**. You can create your résumé using any program you want, but remember that not everyone will be able to open a résumé created in, say, Apple Pages. Even if you use a very common program like Microsoft Word, the formatting can sometimes get lost in translation when you e-mail it to a prospective employer. A better plan is to save your résumé in PDF format. Nearly any potential employer will be able to easily open and view a PDF version of a résumé, and you'll also ensure that your formatting stays intact.

Searching for a Job

It used to be that people looked for jobs in the newspaper. The Sunday classifieds were the place to find employment! That is rarely the case in the Information Age; nowadays, people do most of their job searching online.

There are plenty of job search engines and websites available, and it's certainly worth your time to use those. However, an even better way to look for jobs in the architecture field is to use the American Institute of Architects' online Career Center. That job search platform is focused completely on jobs related to architecture, and you're likely to find a lot more quality jobs there than on a more general job search engine like Monster.com.

Some other job search platforms that specialize in architecture and related jobs include Archinect, Architizer Professional, InternMatch (this one is for internships more than jobs), Coroflot, Arkitectum, and the AIAS (American Institute of Architecture Students) Careers Center. At many of these platforms, you can not only search for jobs but also create an online profile and upload your résumé so employers searching for new hires can find you. If you want to go old school and search the classifieds, you can hop over to *Architect* magazine's website and search their job forum.

Last but definitely not least, *never* underestimate the power of networking. When you meet other people involved in the architectural field, make a connection. If you have a business card, give it to them, or see whether they have a card to give you so you can contact them in the future. Architecture is like many other fields in that often who you know is the key to your future employment.

Glossary

aesthetics Principles concerning beauty, nature, and artistic taste.

anti-Semitism Prejudice against Jewish people.

Baby Boomer Someone born shortly after World War II. The birth rate in the United States rose sharply after World War II, and the babies born during that time were known as part of the "baby boom."

blue-collar Jobs that require manual labor.

Byzantine The eastern part of the Roman Empire during the Middle Ages. The capital was Constantinople, which stood where Istanbul is now. The dominant language of the Byzantine Empire was Greek.

cantilever To fix with a long beam, girder, or bracket on a wall or projection to support a balcony, cornice, or similar structure.

citadel A fortress protecting a city. Citadels were often built on high ground.

corrugated A material shaped into alternating ridges and grooves.

cupola A small dome.

Deconstructivist A movement of postmodern architecture that began in the 1980s that challenges the norms of architectural design and uses unpredictable and sometimes shocking shapes to create a structure.

environmental conservation The desire to preserve the environment and make life more sustainable. Environmental conservationists try to preserve natural resources as much as possible to avoid depleting them.

hieroglyphics Pictures of objects that represent words, syllables, or sounds found in ancient Egyptian and other writing systems.

homage Honor or respect shown publicly.

HVAC An acronym for heating, ventilation, and air conditioning.

indigenous Native or naturally occurring in a particular place.

flying buttress A buttress slanted from a separate pier. Flying buttresses generally form arches with the walls they support.

fresco A style of watercolor painting done on wet plaster of a wall or ceiling. The colors penetrate the plaster and become fixed as the wall or ceiling dries.

lintel A piece of wood or stone that lies across the top of a door or window to hold the weight of the structure above it.

megalith A large stone that forms part of a prehistoric monument.

Mesopotamia An ancient region lying generally in the area of Iraq, between the Tigris and Euphrates Rivers.

monastic Relating to monks and nuns living under religious vows.

pantheistic A religious doctrine that considers God to be the universe or sees the universe as a manifestation of God.

pendentive A curved triangle support that is formed when a dome intersects with its supporting arches.

postmodern Related to a late twentieth-century movement in the arts and architecture. Postmodernism distrusts established theories and ideologies, as well as any definition of "art."

Prairie style An architectural style popular in the late nineteenth and early twentieth centuries commonly found in homes in the Midwest.

Prohibition A time period between 1920 and 1933 in which the manufacture and sale of alcohol was illegal in the United States.

sustainable design The philosophy of designing buildings and other structures with as little negative impact on the natural environment as possible.

trompe l'oeil An illusion in art that tricks the viewer into seeing painted details as three-dimensional objects.

vernacular architecture A style of architecture based on local needs and reflecting local conditions.

white-collar Those who work in an office or other professional environment.

ziggurat A rectangular stepped tower found in ancient Mesopotamia.

Further Information

Books

Bowkett, Steve. *Archidoodle: The Architect's Activity Book.* London: Laurence King Publishing, 2013.

Dillon, Patrick, and Stephen Biesty. *The Story of Buildings: From the Pyramids to the Sydney Opera House and Beyond.* Somerville, MA: Candlewick, 2014.

Salvadori, Mario, and Saralinda Hooker. *The Art of Construction: Projects and Principles for Beginning Engineers & Architects.* Chicago: Chicago Review Press, 2000.

Websites

AIA
aia.org
This website for the American Institute of Architects is primarily for practicing architects, but the site has a useful section for students who are interested in pursuing a career in architecture. It also provides a list of the many universities that have summer architecture programs for high school students interested in learning more.

NCARB
www.ncarb.org
The website for the National Council of Architectural Registration Boards provides up-to-date information on becoming an architect, where to study, how to enroll in the Intern Development Program, and how to get ready for the Architect Registration Examination.

Bibliography

Benavente, Othon. Interview on May 28, 2015.

Berg, Nate. "Should I Start My Own Architecture Firm?" *Architect Magazine.* June 4, 2014. www.architectmagazine. com/business/should-i-start-my-own-architecture-firm_o.

Biography.com. "Frank Gehry." n.d. www.biography.com/ people/frank-gehry-9308278.

Borson, Bob. "Do You Want to Be an Architect?" *Life of an Architect,* n.d. www.lifeofanarchitect.com/do-you-want-to-be-an-architect/.

Boston Architectural College. "Summer Academy: High School Design Exploration."n.d. www.the-bac.edu/education-programs/summer-academy.

Bureau of Labor Statistics, US Department of Labor. "Landscape Architects." *Occupational Outlook Handbook, 2014-15 Edition.* Accessed May 22, 2015. www.bls.gov/ooh/ architecture-and-engineering/landscape-architects.htm.

———. "Architects." *Occupational Outlook Handbook, 2014-15 Edition.* Accessed May 22, 2015. www.bls.gov/ooh/ architecture-and-engineering/architects.htm.

———. "Civil Engineers." *Occupational Outlook Handbook, 2014-15 Edition.* Accessed May 22, 2015. www.bls.gov/ooh/ architecture-and-engineering/civil-engineers.htm.

———. "Drafters." *Occupational Outlook Handbook, 2014-15 Edition.* Accessed May 22, 2015. www.bls.gov/ooh/ architecture-and-engineering/drafters.htm.

———. "Marine Engineers and Naval Architects." *Occupational Outlook Handbook, 2014-15 Edition*. Accessed May 22, 2015. www.bls.gov/ooh/architecture-and-engineering/marine-engineers-and-naval-architects.htm.

Craven, Jackie. "Become an Architect!" About.com. n.d. architecture.about.com/cs/careers/a/bearchitect.htm.

———. "If I Study Architecture, What Is the College Curriculum Like?" About.com. n.d. architecture.about.com/cs/careers/f/collegecurric.htm.

———. "To Be an Architect, What Subjects Should I Take in High School?" About.com. n.d. architecture.about.com/cs/careers/f/archprepare.htm.

———. "What Can I Do with a Major in Architecture?" About.com. n.d. architecture.about.com/cs/careers/f/architectdo.htm.

DesignIntelligence. "America's Best Architecture Schools 2015." January 20, 2015. www.di.net/articles/americas-best-architecture-schools-2015.

Encyclopedia Britannica. "Cliff Dwelling." n.d. www.britannica.com/EBchecked/topic/121493/cliff-dwelling.

———. "I. M. Pei." n.d. www.britannica.com/EBchecked/topic/448812/IM-Pei.

———. "Legion of Honor." n.d. www.britannica.com/EBchecked/topic/335043/Legion-of-Honour.

———. "Prairie Style." n.d. www.britannica.com/EBchecked/topic/473858/Prairie-style.

Encyclopedia of Art. "History of Architecture (3,000 BCE–Present)." n.d. www.visual-arts-cork.com/architecture-history.htm.

Ethnoarchitecture. "Vernacular Architecture." n.d. www. vernaculararchitecture.com.

Glassdoor. "Salary: Architect in San Francisco." n.d. www. glassdoor.com/Salaries/san-francisco-architect-salary-SRCH_ IL.0,13_IM759_KO14,23.htm.

Go Architecture Schools. "A Day in an Architect's Life." n.d. http://www.goarchitectureschools.com/a-day-in-an-architects-life.html.

Greenland.com. "Dwellings of the Inuit Culture: From Igloos to Turf Huts." n.d. www.greenland.com/en/about-greenland/ culture-spirit/hunting-culture/dwellings-of-the-inuit-culture.

Greenwood, Beth. "Architectural Engineer Vs. Architect." *Houston Chronicle.com*. n.d. work.chron.com/architectural-engineer-vs-architect-19557.html.

Guerrini, Federico. "This 'Emergency Floor' Is Going to Make Life Easier for Millions of Refugees." July 6, 2015. *Forbes*. www. forbes.com/sites/federicoguerrini/2015/07/06/low-cost-modular-emergency-floor-could-help-improve-the-lives-of-millions.

Hunter, Michael. "Royal Society." *Encyclopedia Britannica*. August 3, 2014. www.britannica.com/EBchecked/ topic/511584/Royal-Society.

IIT College of Architecture. "Experiment in Architecture." n.d. www.arch.iit.edu/study/experiment-in-architecture.

Kaufmann, Jr., Edgar. "Frank Lloyd Wright." *Encyclopedia Britannica*. n.d. www.britannica.com/EBchecked/ topic/649476/Frank-Lloyd-Wright.

My School of Architecture. "A Typical Day in the Life of an Architect." n.d. myschoolofarchitecture.com/a-typical-day-in-the-life-of-an-architect.

National Council of Architectural Registration Boards. "IDP Intern Development Program Guidelines July 2014." www. ncarb.org/en/Experience-Through-Internships/~/media/ Files/PDF/Guidelines/IDP_Guidelines.pdf.

———. "Intern Development Program." n.d. www.ncarb.org/ experience-through-internships.aspx.

Salary.com. "Architect V Salaries in Omaha, NE." n.d. www1. salary.com/NE/Omaha/Architect-V-salary.html.

Study.com. "Architect: Overview for Starting a Career in Architecture." n.d. study.com/articles/Architect_Overview_ for_Starting_a_Career_in_Architecture.html.

Summerson, Sir John. "Sir Christopher Wren." *Encyclopedia Britannica.* n.d. www.britannica.com/EBchecked/ topic/649414/Sir-Christopher-Wren.

Taliesin Preservation, Inc. "Youth Programs." n.d. www. taliesinpreservation.org/education/youth-programs.

Tempest, Rone. "Controversial New Pyramid Entrance to the Louvre Opens in Paris." *Los Angeles Times.* March 30, 1989. articles.latimes.com/1989-03-30/entertainment/ca-1039_1_ glass-pyramid.

Trynauer, Matt. "Architecture in the Age of Gehry." *Vanity Fair.* August 2010. www.vanityfair.com/culture/2010/08/ architecture-survey-201008?currentPage=all.

University of Notre Dame School of Architecture. "Career Discovery for High School Students." n.d. http://architecture. nd.edu/academics/professional-development/career- discovery.

Index

Page numbers in **boldface** are illustrations. Entries in **boldface** are glossary terms.

About the Author

Cathleen Small is an editor and author who has written numerous books for Cavendish Square. She lives in the San Francisco Bay Area, where she recently bought and renovated a home. When she's not writing or editing, Cathleen enjoys spending time with her sons and traveling.